NIG
A Collecti

Dear Brenda
lots of loves
Tunes in
Soho —
x Alyntte
November 2008

NIGHT BUS
A Collection of Poetry

By
Alyson Hunter

ADELPHI PUBLISHING
LONDON

Published 2008
by Adelphi Publishing,
Heckington, Lincolnshire, UK
NG34 9RA

www.adelphipublishing.co.uk

This First Edition subcribed by
Alexander Charles Ltd.100 Pall Mall, London, UK

Copyright © Alyson Hunter 2008

All rights reserved. No part of this publication may be reproduced, stored in a retrieval system, or transmitted, in any form or by any means, electronic, mechanical, photocopying, recording or otherwise without the prior consent of the publishers and copyright owner.

A CIP catalogue record for this book is available from the British Library.

ISBN 978-0-9558446-0-7

Typeset by Columns Design, Reading RG4 7DH, UK
Printed by T.J. International Ltd, Padstow, Cornwall, UK

Cover photograph © Alyson Hunter 2008

Contents

Meeting Auden 2004	1
Rubber Bullet 2004	2
Lorna 2006	3
Newlyn Quay 1977	4
Lover 1974	5
Cornish Lad 1988	6
Mermaid 1988	8
Under Penzance Promenade 1988	9
Night Beach 1988	10
Walking Back 1976	11
Morrab Gardens at Night 1988	12
To my Mother in Law 1988	13
Penzance Promenade 1979	14
The Fan Letter 1988	15
North Corner 1979	16
Folsom Blues 1981	17
New York 1981	18
Perspective 1983	20
California 1981	21
The Bumpkins 2007	22
Whisky Christmas 1987	23
Underground 1988	24
Barrel of Laughs 1987	26
Spilt Water 1986	27
Guilt 1988	28
Goodbye 1988	29
Newlyn Harbour 1988	30

Bedclothes 1988	31
Holloway 1990	32
Art Dealer 1986	33
Park Swings 1985	34
Saturday Night 1988	35
Woman's Prison 1986	36
Snow 1988	37
London Buddleia 1988	38
Rabbit 1989	40
Impulsion 1988	41
Alikeness 1988	42
Gulf War 1990	43
Asian London 1986	44
Night Words 1988	45
Telephone Call 1999	46
The Borrowed Coat 2004	47
Married Man 2004	48
Stranger 1995	49
The Coffee pot 1999	50
Elphic 2002	51
Kate 1998	52
Spaceship Drink 2004	53
Ice 2004	54
Picnic 2004	55
Mr. Alcohol 2004	56
Purple 2004	58
Clone 2004	59
Missing 2004	60
Text Me 2004	61
Leopards 2004	62

Shunt 2004	63
Chaos 2004	64
Silent Night 2004	65
Veeraswamy 2003	66
Colours 2004	68
Dishcloth 2005	69
My Muse 2004	70
Spanish Sun 2004	72
Vanunu 2005	73
It was all my Fault 2004	74
Ireland 2004	76
Voices 2004	77
Camden 2005	78
Wave 2005	79
Far Away 2004	80
Beloved 2005	81
Walking in the City 2005	82
The Northern Wind 2005	83
A Country Childhood 2005	84
The Stream 2005	85
The Lamplighter 2005	86
Night Bus 2005	88
Kentish Town 1995	89
The Master of Ceremonies 2004/5	90
Armed 2006	92
Struggle 2005	93
Lash 2005	94
Sunflower 2004	95
Regents Park 2005	96
The Turning Tree 2005	97

Tower block 2005	98
Whitebait 2005	99
Cut-out 2005	100
An English Field 2004	101
St. George Flag 2005	102
To Seamus Heaney 2004	104
Like Me 2004	105
Poesy 2006	106
Poetry Reading 2004	107
Chuff 2005	108
Love at First sight 2005	109
Kentish Town Tree 2006	110
Ant Heads 2006	111
To A Child of Suicide 2006	112
Hazlitt's Hotel 2005	113
Lilies 2005	114
Torture 2006	115
Yellow and Orange 2006	116
Landsdowne Club 2005	117
Published 2005	118
Kentish Town Night 2006	119
Brakes 2006	120
El Peurto de Santa Maria 2006	121
Opening 2006	122
Pegs on the line 2006	123
Night Troubled 2006	124
Girl 2006	125
Christopher 2006	126
Street Tree 2007	127

Meeting Auden

Just the two of us,
in an Oxford tea shop,
his face a craggy cliff,
the eyes jewelled creatures
hiding in the crevices.

I thought of hanging in there
from a small tree
with one hand,
the human clay crumbling
from my desperate foothold–
'Help, help', I would cry

He smiled encouragingly at me,
the quiet girl in the corner
too shy to speak–
'Oh let me fall, let me talk to strangers!'

Or perhaps I did fall,
into that youthful abyss of;
'Who does he think he is, anyway?'

Rubber Bullet

In a Brixton basement gathered
a coven of male witches
intensely justified
around their cauldron of civil rights,
making the air in the room constrict–
as if the English were listening in.
They had something to show me.
Suddenly like a newborn babe
cradled in their pale hands
was a rubber bullet.
I cried out
'It is so black!
It is so big!
It is so hard!'
I heard the child in my voice
felt the vast racist fear of my parents
looming behind me,
suddenly, unconsciously
at the sight of
the obscene
organ of peacekeeping.

Lorna

Oh Lorna, Lorna, where are you now?
Reading Lorna Doone to each other,
the sun so hot we couldn't see the page.
Your father would have you married early,
centuries, worlds apart from each other we were–
but then you were as the glossy brown pips
in my white apple heart, Lorna Green.

Newlyn Quay

As I lie on the Old Quay
my soft white body
is warm against the hard granite.

Am I resting where
coarse red hands
have pulled wet metal chains
and rough sepia ropes?
Has a drowned man lain
where I lie now?

His wife was still waiting and hoping
but his blind mistress
has taken him deep
into her cold green sheets,
soothing him with her icy arms,
seducing his bold red to white,
caressing his body
with the slow movement
of crashing storm
and sucking tide.

Lover

As time forfeits love
each sunlit hour passes
without your lover's touch,
each others lifetimes crossing
on different turning paths,
each simple moment lasting
of awakened life and sleep,
neither agony nor pleasure,
measured by
love's bitter keep.

Cornish Lad

Whomsoever, your Cornish darkness?
Was it when swarthy Phoenicians traded
in your river mouths
or when the fierce Spaniards
chopped and enslaved you?
A dark human pike
sprung deep into the heart
of Mousehole's white and sheltered cove.

I see it in the length of your lashes
and the darkness of the dark curl
that hangs across your black eyes.
Your limbs hang proud and loose,
for you are confident in your manliness
and the strength for outside work.

Do I love you because of this?
Or is it because, the salt water
of the murky Manukau
mixes well with the mackerel waters
of this curving harbour of Marazion?
Mine kissed by a hotter rain
than floats over this seaside town.

Now if I should place
my pallid pawn
across the chequered board
and let my native king
be abounded by your queenly crown
I shall be a vanquished victress then.

For even if so quickly checked by you
I have made you play this game of war
where no blood is spilled outright,
even though mix it might,
on this,
this silent Cornish night.

Mermaid

If only one could give up
these shards of glass
one is treading on
these wishes and dreams.

Rather to die
and return to the sea
for my limbs are divided
and walking is agony.

>Oh, to be whole again
>to just be as one,
>to feel safe, to be
>not fragmented
>and not long,
>hopelessly,
>for my
>tail.

Under Penzance Promenade

The enormous gulls stalk the leaden shore
the sky sits sullen against the edge
of the ponderous sea
with its still sheen of sateen
the hot breeze stirs saltant
and moves the hair across my gaze
as if I am the moving picture show
and the rest some odd reality
some land in past or future
once glimpsed in the imagination
attuned to the wireless
lost in space, fighting with shadows
long ago
escaping the raw tedium
of the existent place
and my temporal self.

Night Beach

The sea waves sheen up rippling smooth
black silk stockings on large black thighs
stretching out to the night sky and beyond–
a girdle of white pearls
rushes up to the edge of the hips
to foam gently on the lip
of the triangle of dusky sand
sculptured by the rounding waves.

Walking softly on her yielding belly
towards the lights of Newlyn shining out
I see gold coins sprinkled on a bed of black velvet
as if Zeus has been and gone,
and his shower has quieted the night air,
as the black girl of Newlyn sleeps.

Walking Back

The spreading bruise of the day
purples the swelling water
within the rhythm
the seabirds call a morning cry
soft, careful, over the salt-bitten heather.

The road shines with the moon and the morning
her white face smiling blind
above the curve
of the Cornish sea.

Arm in arm, the women
stumble from Mousehole
walking to Penzance,
exclaiming at the warm waking birds,
the frosty flowers, the proud boats
bobbing black within
the stone breast of Newlyn.

The women laugh, to be free
like the reflections in the sea waves
together, and yet away,
together, and yet free.

Distracted, for a moment
from that consuming love
of men and children.

Morrab Gardens at Night

The half-moon hangs in the curve
of a Prussian blue sky, a disembodied light
as abstract as the night-time seagulls' cry,
and the tolling of the Penzance bell for midnight.

The tree waves its lacy blackness in the wind
as the golden sulphur streetlight
lights up the body of the trunk;
as if a beautiful woman leans
by a yellow party light.

The cars nuzzle the flank of the stone wall
and far Newlyn glitters with fanciful twinkling
between the darkened leaves.

Speculate that the moonlight is tangible
solidly lighting the velvety blackness
between the flowers and palms–
who are murmuring between themselves
against the injustices of the day.

To My Mother-in-Law

I have left your basket of fruit upon my doorstep.
You watch it–
sometimes it rots,
at other times it takes on strange luxurious growth,
spiky pineapple blaze, plump redness of bursting plum–
but it doesn't wither and die,
unwatered, as you thought.

You want to take him back into your strong arms,
close to your bosom,
use your powerful mothers mind–
and smash my doorstep.
I do sometimes smile from the window
but I never come over to your side of the street–
cross over your stoop–
and if I gave him back,
your basket of fruit would shrink and fade,
because your milk is tainted with possession,
and your breasts would fill with burrs.

Penzance Promenade

We walked along the promenade,
and lent on the cold white rail.
You looked at the sea,
an infinite cup of light,
saucered in porcelain blue,
with a rim of soft silver.
I thought you would say
'Is this not beautiful?'
But you said to my surprise–
'You do not belong here,
it is too small for you'.
And then
'Have I lost you?'
and I answered in a small voice
'Yes', to your pallid face.

Ten years later, on the promenade
the sea and the sky
clenched like a black woollen fist
around the string of golden lights,
as if all the night had withdrawn itself from me.
I missed your companionship,
and was sorry I said yes,
so truthfully that day.
But my heart had to ride the storm
and test its timbered keel
in search of foreign lands–
even then to return here
an empty-handed sailor,
with that exotic knowledge
seen only in the narrowed eye.
Always to be apart
from those so safely ashore.

The Fan Letter

My only fan letter
came from Memphis, Tennessee
Official Business, Department of Justice
Cell no. six-three-three.
The inmate here had written:

'Sixteen years ago I killed a grown man
with my fists when only eighteen.
I was to die by electrocution,
but now I have life in prison.
From your painting
I look from within my own dark forest–
I see touches of loveliness
and brilliance outside these shadows,
I cannot begin to describe the wealth of feeling
which your art evokes in me,
It's as if I have fallen in love.'

This man did not know
that our mothers make
with their whisperings and touching
a stronger prison to echo
the wired caged corset
of their mother's Victorian repression–
painted wooden Russian dolls
dresses locking over and hiding each smaller female figure
and so the light shining through my work
was the shedding of that tainted blackness
and the golden dawn of
my own adulthood.

North Corner

I will now never
feel the warmth of your hearth,
face the summer sea wind
on your balcony.
I have thought about your every beam,
planted flowers around you,
painted your windows blue,
pointed your granite walls,
bathed in your enclosed light
you have seen me in every moment,
of happiness and despair,
stood still and shocked
as I showed the secrets
of my naked body
to lustful eager eyes. Yes,
you hold my guilty secrets
where I have none.
Why don't you plead with me
to keep you?
Or in your silence
do I hear jealousy,
of my need to leave you,
and to love other houses, far away.

Folsom Blues

The ex-prisoners got on the dusty bus outside the prison,
the air electric with the smell of constraint–
their muscular bodies still cowed by hurt,
watchful, noticing everything, not looking,
wanting every mile away to be gone away
so Greyhound fast, to get out of there.

My baby started screaming hot and thirsty
politely they offered their bottles to me
I torn asunder by her sobs
still refused, for
my mother long ago
a bonny baby in a pram,
was dealt a poisonous kiss
by a cruel witch unknown to all
a quick revenge on new life
a curse forever upon her lips.

So we all rode away from Folsom,
with my baby crying,
the sound of small freedoms first heard,
to jar this reflective company of men,
away and up the great Route Eighty–
all of us hostages to our past.

New York

In the bath, in the refrigerator door, sleeping on the walls
the cockroaches squat, as if to say
'Go home, this is our town'.
I go down to the basement
through the fetid air of the Chelsea hotel–
the Puerto Ricans smirk when I ask for roach spray–
for sprayed roaches just grow bigger, and lick their lips,
and clean their glossy wings again.

I put the bedside light on, and read
'I love you', written in blood
illuminated on the underneath of the lampshade.
Next door, a crocodile is kept in the bath.
Why is that woman screaming in the hall?

I scamper through the snow,
the city so alive around me,
I kick the yellow leaves in Washington Square,
as drunks girdle under skeleton trees–
the brownstone buildings surround us,
black fists clenched as if against us.

The mournful bear in Central Park stares
at the bedraggled monkey, mad with boredom,
as she shakes the rusty bars back and forth,
and the weekend fathers watch
clasping silent children.

Downtown I walk under the towers and an eerie gust
of cold wind frightens me away
their tops swim in the sky, so straight, so sightless
I run, pushing the pram to safety.

Walking on Green Street
I know I will never see this New York again
I love the European decay
for one day it will be–
American, clean, striving
easy and rich, but that's all right.

Perhaps I am too romantic–
I cry for the poverty-stricken Santa Claus
in his ragged red robes and yellowed beard
on Seventeenth Street, his bell,
a leper's bell clanging
New York,
New York.

Perspective

My students hovered close
'Professor', they said, 'we want to say'.
Silence, then one spoke
'We don't think you are a professor, Professor.'

'Shall I grow a moustache for you?'
I asked, taken aback.
'No Professor, we don't mean that at all.'
Their eyes were like the walnuts,
the hard Californian walnuts,
that grew in lines, tight long miles,
up to the hazy mountains.
Then they said earnestly
'You are too like us.' they said,
'You think too young.'

'Get back to work,' I said.
'I think you should study,
and so really understand,
the perspective of clouds.'

California

A child was murdered
there, in the school playground.
the locals murmured
the Klu Klux Klan.
For he was from somewhere
like South Vietnam.

In the Davis Mall
the jolly lady at the till
said, with her pleasant drawl,
'Well, they shouldn't come here
Why do they come here,
from South Vietnam?'

I guess somebody sent her son
in a troop carrier to some place,
kissed and hugged him goodbye,
some time ago, somehow.
Some lad.
To somewhere else.

Everyplace just someplace
that is not here,
a bad dream, there,
don't go to sleep again,
sleepy California.

The Bumpkins

They walked up that soulless American Road,
with the sightless cars and trundling trucks
as high as buildings,
to a smoky cheap hotel.
Mr. Bumpkin asked how much the rooms were.
The brothel men were rather astounded
but herded them into the rickety lift and
Mrs Bumpkin smelt death as the three men
sized up Mr. Bumpkin, a foot higher than them
and country-swim muscled
but no match for wolves–
so she said over their baby's head–
'We will have to get our money and come back
to take a room', so they went down in the lift
the men not having time to make a plan.

Back on the road walking quickly away
they were followed by a lame lady,
who said 'Come back' – and aside to Mrs. Bumpkin–
'they will kill you both, but they won't harm the baby'.
Mr. Bumpkin said 'What a friendly place,
we should stay there'.
Now Death was there, black and lean, laughing so much
he had to lean on his pitchfork,
the dusty trucks pounding behind him–
but all was silent
as he went back to the hotel
to play cards with his devilkin.
The family walked away
and Mrs. Bumpkin knew he would
always have games for them,
as long as there was a Mr. and Mrs. Bumpkin.

Whisky Christmas

Oh the baubles on the Christmas tree
sparkle spangle as we shake the presents–
listening for the whisky wetly sounding,
golden heavy in its secret wrapping.

Is it bad luck to open presents early?
Because husbands end up shouting
'Her!
Her! She is not the intellectual
of this house–
she is a big black spider sitting there.'

The guest, drunk, falls over the tree,
its little arms bravely defend itself
as it crashes greenly to the ground.
'Why bother with a silly tree?' he says
It is so small, why bother?'

'Why bother indeed, my lover,'
I whisper through my silken web
as I clench my furred legs tight together
surrounded by your whisky breaths
and the misery of Christmas.

You want to tear at my fragile
sticky strands,
but I will eat you both,
one day, one day.

Underground

She is a dormouse scurrying,
to lick up the breadcrumbs
from under my table–
with her desperate doormat love.
I could, with one flick,
drag the carpet she is scrubbing
at so lovingly
right from under her knees.
If I really wanted him.
Dear Mary Woollenscroft, it is sad
that the blood of serving girls
still runs strong in some of us still.

I will go down now
into my dark world, my underground,
darkness of dreams, soot smell of the past,
where Orpheus searches, uniformed,
his wan face handsome in the half-light,
now partner in the depths
to Hercules–
who accepts the tickets with steady grasping.
Hark there is Cerberus
jaws straining to the light outside,
blind barking, never to be carried up.
Hades' majestic voice warns
'Mind, mind the gap.'

But I fell there a long time ago,
and now like Persephone I will go down
in this iron cage,
and my heart
will never return as Kore
to the world of Dementa–
it is too bleak, if sunny on occasion,
and in these echoing caverns I will learn to love myself,
I need not now ever look back,
for there is nothing but my own memories
floating like dust in the sunlight.

Barrel of Laughs

Silver light through sunlit squares,
golden whisky smoothly glides,
wet beer blearily bubbles,
smoke edges around
the wet tables.

The green baize,
a brightly lit grass,
coloured clicking balls,
bared teeth a white flash,
wolfish laughter.
'What a card!
Must be a barrel of laughs to live with.'

That somebody quiet could drown in
like a kingly queen,
white face floating,
down under the purple
haze of sickly sweet malmsey,
with no hands pushing down,
just sinking,
alone and unaided.

Spilt Water

The water spilt, changed shape
rushed away, and my fault went too–
I gave up, it was as if
the last of my tears had
just splashed on the ground,
with all the wasted love, all the pain of it,
down the path, around the wall,
down to the harbour, into the sea.

The sea with the little bobbing boats
sailing on the expanse of calm blue.
Out there, away from all this.

A little hand timidly took mine
'Look at the pretty boats' I said.
It was going to be all right
One day it would be just us alone
after a long, hard, time.

Guilt

At night when the mind should slumber
guilt creeps into dreams
and you wake suddenly
in a cell of your own making.

He used to start in his sleep
he thought his daylight hours
with his philandering child-like needs
were undiscovered, unknown to me.

So his agony on awakening
and the tossing of his limbs
were those of a traitor in an enemy's camp
a slave would not have dared move so–
as if a sword was hacking at the bed
on which we lay.

Now I feel guilt from another's kiss,
and drink from another's cup,
he and I both dream sweet quietness, neutralized,
slumbering as two warriors spent.
The war can rage outside
but we have had our years together
before all this,
and dreams can feed on only memories,
slipping back to the days
when the enemy was without
and not within,
and so we rest, once more,
just this last time, together enfolded
in a family shape.

Goodbye

You say you don't want to be with me,
you want happiness.
I can't give you what you crave,
only your mother can give you that–
you are a fool
in a baby's dress.
If you seek that happiness
in such a one as me
you will be lost forever–
anyone that cares to look for my soul
will find in my unhappiness
life in its small realities,
and everyday things will appear
great in their splendour.

So therefore, you should
not mantel this mate
with your need for success,
but succour my talent
wandering through the
hills of obscurity.

Forsake me, then
for I have no goals,
no male fantasies of hopeless height,
every day has its pleasures for me–
go now and walk the
wide waters of ambition–
I taste success always
with the tip of my tongue,
and when you have caught your loaf and fish,
you will wander in the desert of loneliness,
because you once knew me.

Newlyn Harbour

Is love wrecked upon this rounded quay?
From whence launched naked brown muscle
in drunken bravado, as
straight and swift as a human torpedo
into the greasy sea.

Disappearing, then like Pan arising
behind the orange iron of the new pier
with the trawler men's relieved laughter,
to shock the matrons of Newlyn Strand–
because we hid his clothes
in the little trawler's cabin.

Looking now, ten years on,
is this all that is left?
these ribbons of tawny weed,
translucent green and brittle tawny ochre,
threaded amongst the grey dappled stones
whose edges are worn
a little more than on that day.

Bedclothes

Our bedclothes lie in rips
ready for the slash of my spent paintbrush
they still smell faintly of your body
and all those long ago dreams
in a small room four floors up.

This cloth did see happiness
of a family sort, young hopes
the cherubic baby limbs, the sweetest smile
our animated talking
the dreams spilling out of the high windows.

I remember you eager
red against the cool chintz flowers
a white breast, dark hair
and laughter.

The dreams dashed upon the ground
for they where the crazy dreams of youth
and we betrayed
what we had
just for dreams, silly dreams.

Holloway

What strength I had then
to withstand the steady roar
of your rubber and diesel soul–
a ceaseless driven drive
under suicide bridge,
a bridge so glamorously high–
but you will never claim me.

I gritted my teeth
against that cold English fume,
amongst my fellow foreigners,
as the prison walls seep
unseen degradation
palpable in the shadows
of this nadir of a road.

Your hollow shape was made
by the dusty hoof, the beasts
driven to slaughter,
down to the knives of Smithfield–
the sweat and steam rising
from the heaving flanks with
the keening of low terror.

Returning here, I can only be grateful
that I could look after my own,
and marvel at my dogged spirit
to inch away, to survive
this tacky noisy nowhere.

Art Dealer

I said, 'I like a man with an appetite.'
You even ate the food from my plate–
your smart suit strained with your Irish fun,
as we kissed in the cool of the British Museum.
You said to me aghast,
'Why do you live like a student? '
and, 'You have to understand,
selling art is ninety per cent publicity.'

Then you shot yourself in the head
you hurt your people- I saw their pale faces
under the false heaven of Olympia,
your heaven, full of guilty holes.

I am still a student
studying the various arts
I have kept my head,
and my student's heart.
Not so your Irish fun
that you took
with your Irish gun.

Park Swings

In a drab Islington park,
as we push our daughters on the swings,
the dark-haired woman with the pale face
says, 'No man has ever said
I love you, to me.'
I am shocked, and the silence comes,
between the squeaking of the swings.

I am silent as I think
I have heard I love you,
many times, and yet
never believed the words.
I believe the love
in their troubled eyes
it is the you I do not know.
Is it a mirror held up
for them to love themselves?
Or a void that takes away
their very spirit?
My mother said,
'They see you as a mist,
then you are gone.'

I shrug in answer
as the swings squeak I-love-you
in the silence
of our daughter's steadfast air
'Push harder,' they say,
so sure
that we are there.

Saturday night

The window is a yellow rectangle of light,
within, black silhouettes move about
in time to the beating music.
People enjoying themselves,
on Saturday night.

He says, noticing my interest in the window,
scornfully, enviously,
'What about your art?
'Your art is but between parties.'
'No,' I answer guilelessly
'My art does not stretch enough between parties'.

This Camden pavement here before us
so black and wet, burned through the middle
by a yellow sulphuric stream of light,
spangled by the pale yellow leaves of October,
hailing the new winter in their downward fall.

The whole an Ensor puzzle
positive black, negative yellow
then reversed–
fragments of this Saturday night.
Where am I?
Yellow headlamps light up my black coat
once black, now yellow.
Art I only, only art,
between parties.

Women's Prison

Though the library window,
near the children's books,
overlooking the prison grounds,
I see her grey prison shift,
her face so pale.

A thin body rigid with grief,
hands outstretched
to the uniformed men,
surrounding her- staying back,
on their heels.

'My Baby, my baby' she cries–
her hands shake towards me
as the warder talks her slowly
into bowed submission,
and she is led away.

Behind me in the library
the local women mutter
'Disgusting bitch–
they have a swimming pool,
table tennis you know,
the Life of Riley–
worse than the men they are'.

Their anger cowers me,
I shut my book,
and walk outside
to the free fresh air
of the Camden Road.

Snow

His boots are set in the snow
on the balcony.
I watch his shape through the frosted glass,
as he sits barefoot on the very edge–
everything outside looks very Christmas,
five floors below.

His eyes are glazed
and he won't go away.

He is not here
he has jumped
his broken body
lies like a twisted star
far below
in the whitest snow.
The police surround him
at a distance, a blue circle,
as if he were a wounded scorpion.

They come up to me and say
'Don't worry
It's the area for it.'
The locals say 'We will kill
them anyway, drugs around here.'
But I see my neighbour's
hard face wet with tears.

Snow falls softly like a mother's kiss
and his best cocaine.

London Buddleia

Buddleia grow fat and purple
with swarms of acrid curving clusters
soft against your bitter-tongued leaves,
those swaths of coarse leaf furred
turning on sap-filled stem bristling
from the concrete of this London
I should not love.

The city here shows an ugly face
hard and brutal in this old East end corner
but allows succour to you, Buddleia
to flower through soot, striving so gay
gently bowing in the rain.

Like you, my blood is filled
with the grit of this place
that my Huia mosquitoes would spit
from their curling mouths
that I would, and cannot.
Blood gritted and thinned forever
mauve with English light
but always foreign, like you, flower.

I, the mosquitoes would feast thirstily on now
so I can never return to the Huia of my past,
waiting for Father Christmas in the back of the Holden,
all through the sleepless sweaty night–
even the cicada silent,
no footsteps or sleigh-ride jingle,
only the carol call whine
of your deadly feeding

my skin and blood never thick enough
imprisoned by the promise of a beach-sand ride
on Huia's old donkey.

Like him I am stubborn enough
to cling to the streets of London,
and strive so gay in the pouring rain
to wait always for footsteps,
and for Father Christmas.

Rabbit

I sit slumped on the sofa,
watching the television.
Simon comes up to me,
touching me with his paw
warm, wanting company.
I stroke him,
him, so animal, so bestial.
I look him in the eyes
eyes so dark, so unfathomable.
He is just there, close,
a presence in a fur overcoat,
yet genteelly naked.
Perhaps he understands–
he does not have to speak,
perhaps he loves me.
We sit together, his nose on my arm
together silent.
I speak to him, 'I love you,
you know I do,
Simon.'
But I cannot read those eyes of his,
or hope to understand.

Impulsion

You move towards me though the crowd,
as I set my face in a mask of indifference.
You turn away and I immediately grieve–
I feel as if I were a doe deep in the forest
mortally wounded,
struck by a crossbow bolt,
standing in pain, silent in the darkening glade.
Impulsively, I turn to follow you with my eyes
and you turn to me and say 'Let's go'.

But it was too strong a start for me,
I retreated,
gratefully waking in the room of my past,
alone, the battleground still abandoned
in the morning light, the frosted blades
of grass still unbroken,
all unstained by the pulse of love,
that would cost us both too dear.

Alikeness

I watched my child growing,
her father's child, with long golden limbs,
with eyes as brown as burnt toffee,
and sometimes a doughy English look about her face,
that with time, grew less and less.

But her gaze belonged to me,
a long scornful look from darkened brow.

In the pub we sat with pen and paper,
writing on the table wet ringed with beer.
Then she got up, and was seen outside
through the patterned pane of the dusty window.

As she looked up and wrote out the letters of the sign,
the sunlit petals of her face
flew apart and regrouped again.

Hair hairgrips glimmered gold,
as her head moved to and fro
in the glassy squares.
At every earnest movement
her image flew distractedly away,
and melded back again
with studious desire.

And then I knew her soul
was as mine, all mine.

Gulf War

I am from Simon de la How
De Bareworth, Abingdon, and Hungerford,
Congleton, Macclesfield, Stockport and Hampton.
Who at Ascalon overcame
three Saracen chiefs in single combat.
So three crescent moons
are born by his descendants
won fair, by bravery and skill
glorifying religious invasion.

Now with armoured steeds of the air,
faster, unseen, tearing at the sky
in the soft light of their crescent moon
dealing modern smoke and fury–
I wish no Christian vengeance–
unease, unease is what I feel
when we gloat over these
fireworks of death
from our sofas.

Blood swells the sand again
over the smothered army
of Saddam's frightened recruits
not fought hand to hand
or eye to eye
so everything burning
as the oil smoulders
to ignite again–
underneath
this raging storm.

Asian London

Your little wife scurries
three steps behind you
in the underground
buffeted by heavy white shoulders
down in the London tunnels.

Your back is set rigid
as you face the pressing throng
you don't look back for her
she will disappear into the crowd of us–

as the tide is against you–
unless you go arm in arm
you will not get through
this armoured isle.

Night Words

One late night we were talking together
and in the brown cavernous deep
of my mind's thoughts drifting
the words you were speaking
strode starkly like white figures
chalked against a warm fire-lit wall,
stiff male figures marking some prehistoric cave
as when first seen by modern eye-
and I felt then
you are not one of us after all,
these were alien words you spoke
bitter and tight lipped
foreign to me
and the friends of my mind.
I did not hear them well at all
I just knew they were wrong
all together
marching between us, forever.

Telephone Call

He said on the telephone
'I will kill myself,
unless you come over.'

I asked him
'Do I fancy some
Rigor Mortis?'

I may seem hard,
but he doesn't know,
I have just seen him,

in his big car,

        driving

                around,

                        laughing.

The Borrowed Coat

I borrowed a red coat off a city girl,
formal, not quite me.
I stood in the French, nothing was normal,
he said champagne at Kettners?
The red coat said 'Yes, rather!'

Six years later we knew each other,
shyly asleep again in the Groucho, secret lover,
but it was a borrowed red coat, not me,
and so I now bow out,
in my own coat, so much later.

Married Man

If you are in love with a married man
you wish you could rip it from
your hurting heart,
and seal it in an envelope,
and file it under
Lost Loves.

But you are bad at filing,
and this file marked
Hope
should read
Stupid
in your hurting hoping heart.

Stranger

I saw you in the middle of my road,
sobbing, like some broken dinosaur,
all age-furred and foreign,
in your American clothes.

I was astounded at the absence
of the love, that
I had felt so keenly,
so hurtfully, once.
It was if I had
been poisoned, and
was now made well, at last.

I took you inside my house,
and said to our daughter
'Why did you not open the door
to Daddy?'
She replied, 'Remember Mummy,
you told me–
never to answer the door to strangers'.

The Coffee Pot

I make the coffee and remember you.

You said 'You don't love me enough,
and you don't always think of me.
All you want from Radnor Walk
is the shopping in the King's Road.'

You kissed me and saw the coffee pot,
adding, 'You see, a new package here,
when I have been pacing the room,
waiting for you.'

But you were wrong–
I bought the coffee pot
when my thoughts were full of you,
us, drinking coffee,
together.

As I make the coffee for one,
more than anything else,
I am reminded of you,
and your young death.

Elphic

Mick and I went on the Lam, and
Soho disappeared.
We fell over in the hall,
our coats were too heavy,
we were pleased to be safe.

We woke in the morning,
with people walking over us
going to work.
He said, 'We are berthed well like
two tugs snug in a harbour.'

We got up and went to the pub
he was drinking too much,
but the show must go on.
I pleaded with him
'Why?'
He answered,
with tears in his eyes–

'I just love it so much.'

Kate

The doctor asks 'Relative or friend?'
'Friend, I answer, assured of that truth,
thinking of those happy times in your company,
the wry gaiety that sprung between us.

My hands are sweating in the surgical gloves,
but I do not dare to touch your fragile arm
with it's plastic tubes snaking up
between us.

The grime of Camden Town, my very breath
may contaminate you,
taking away this friendship forever.
Yes, my rude health
is a monster in this room.

It cannot empathise with your pain–
it is not sharing, as a friend should.
You despair, as I despair at my uselessness.
Us both still and quiet,
abounded about
by the electricity of death.

Spaceship Drink

So you are calling from Spaceship Drink,
looking for a friendly planet
to come down on,
as you are hurtling, spinning,
out of control.

I, too, used to travel to the stars,
saw those wondrous sights,
be risen up in the Glad Vortex,
to be a God amongst the Meteorites.

Sorry to disappoint you,
I have sadly given up space travel,
and have come to rest
on Planet Normal–
so bugger off
to the Lonely Planet Sphere.

Ice

He said, 'Hell itself
must have frozen over
for you to have
stopped drinking.'

No, it was Heaven I see,
golden, unattainable,
swimming lazily beneath
the icy film,
so brittle
beneath my feet.

So happily you swim there
golden, unattainable,
not knowing me, not caring–
as if you ever did.

Picnic

At a picnic in Hyde Park,
the fountains were gorgeous,
spring sun warmed the skin.
I looked down
at the scuffed grass,
and it brought me bad thoughts–
schooldays,
dislocation, loneliness, boredom,
and me being very hopeless
at catching a ball.
So I got up
brushed off the grass,
and took the tube
to a room in Soho–
gaiety, laughter, friendship,
and me being very expert
at getting quietly drunk.

Mr. Alcohol

God it was so beautiful, our love in Heaven,
with all the stars shining on our happiness.
I could fall into your wonderful world
at the touch of a glass,
you were always waiting, for me alone–
Mr. Alcohol.

Entwined in lover's limbs, locked in languid bliss,
we danced so slow for decades,
no other man could loosen your hold,
my true, trusted companion–
Mr. Alcohol.

Then you became unfaithful, your promises hollow,
you abandoned me, and yes, I admit
I chased you, I stalked you, and I went to your places.
I had no shame; I was not myself,
you with that other woman–
Mr. Alcohol

I could not believe our love had died,
how you despised me, and beat me down
to show me, you didn't care,
and you ever had.
Now you dangle the Decree Absolute
near my hand
Come on, you sneer,
You know you want me,
Just one sip, and you will be free.

But the Decree Nisi is nice, darling,
awfully all right.
And this way, creep, you cannot marry
another poor sister, sucker.
For you have lost your looks, but I know,
underneath, your snakelike charm lives on,
my dear, deadbeat husband,
Mr. Alcohol.

Purple (With apologies to Jenny Joseph)

When I am an old woman,
I will still be purple,
all my money will be laagered,
drunk with a face-lift pretty,
perfecting the form of youthful failings–
throwing up on public railings.

You, man, can take Viagra,
and test your heart with its daily dogma,
and drink even more vile sherry
on your bad stomach, for tea,
and then inject yourself in the arse
with Vitamin B.

Now we must work the blankest page,
and sob and shout on the stage,
for we will just have to manage,
and laugh at other's coarse badinage,
write nervous in the Northern light,
and try each other until a fight.

But before we are suck-tooth rants,
and laugh pissing in our pants
let us not die, with humdrum humble,
as onwards we blindly stumble,
aghast, hand in hand
into grim Old Aged Land.

Clone

I say 'I want to see you,
I need you.'
You reply, 'I am doing this, doing that–
I should be a clone–
everybody wants me!'

'Oh yes, Mighty Sir, then
which one
shall I tell
to *Fuck off?'*

Missing

Missing
my baby girl, now so tall.
Missing
my Mum and Dad and their bad cooking.
Missing
my sisters, forever talking, talking.
Missing
my men, with their strong sure hands on the steering wheel,
driving other women, along other roads, in far-away countries.
Missing I am. Always missing too.
Missing, and now, damn, I'm missing you.

Text Me

Keep the faith, you texted.

Now my telephone is silent,
the silence stretches the miles between us,
my faith is lost
somewhere on the last roundabout,
and Vanessa is more famous than me.
But am I too nervous
to text
Is it all over?
But I did.
And you texted back
All we have is time.

You will have time, to regret,
for you should know
faith is, has to be,
a one-way street.

Leopards

He said to me sternly
'The leopard has changed,
he is not a crazy man anymore,
he has fallen on his feet
with a posh bird,
and he is very happy.'

I feel warned off
and answer him
'It will never happen friend,
wait and see,
when the leopard's spots change,
then, sir, I will
worry for him.'

Survival skills,
they always fuck us up–
and keep us alive.
So alive.

Shunt

You have shunted me off the road
like an old car.

When you are next driving
with your hands clenched on another wheel,
with the smell of a more plastic upholstery,
remember the excitement
of my familiar unfamiliar landscapes,
and how safe you felt inside.

Chaos

You have charming ways that cheered my days
hiding the deep chasm that lay hidden
under your wives' sad midden.

I now play with chiasmus blue
and you are now alone with her,
and she is now alone, so alone, with you.

Silent Night

The DJ and I lay on the bed
with some E
to listen to some sounds
we couldn't move
to put the music on
and became basking crocodiles
on a silent riverbank.

Veeraswamy

The waiters were kind on my birthday
my father would have called them-'nigger-wallas,'
but understood them in his way,
known the gentle eyelashes,
black moths fluttering
against the golden skin.

The metal of the knife and fork
taints the gentle food I long to touch–
'The foreign muck,' you might have said,
but you never ate it, never tried.

You did treasure something–
a long bullet, chrome plated–
as I caressed it, you explained
your friend once owned it.

'Had children, a wife, and cancer, so,
he walked away from his car, kept walking,
in the desert, and the kookaburras watched him die.'
I heard the respect in your voice and understood.

Daddy
in a concrete room, terrible, terrible
with the 'Loonies, nutters,'
you would have called them–
cast down to animal with Alzheimer's
bedevilled by Dementia, hosed down,
eyes bulging, starved to skeleton
in a skeleton hell, a cold inferno
a cruel zoo, where respect is a savage word.

I swallow hard, and think of my mother's stricken face
her saying she didn't know those awful places existed.
Of course they do, they do.
We only respect the well.

So I would cast my lot with you, if you would have me,
black moths, for I wager,
you would not force-feed a dying man, and here is
a silver tear for the golden champagne,
as the velvet night darkens
the windows of Veeraswamy.

Colours

So, Joe, Conrad, you write,
'A black man with white features
is the Devil's work.'
I say
like very white men
with very black hair–
too witch-like by half.

And orange-haired people
with transparent skin,
their freckles
floating on the surface.

And arrogant blondes
with red scurvy flush,
from too many pies,
and fries.

Ken ye, Conrad, white husks
Keeping no spiritualism,
Knowing no compassion,
in their hollow eyes.

Closing up the fear
underneath the colour
of us all.

Dishcloth

Your dishcloth is not dirty
but if I was
to take it out into the street,
people would pay
to have it caged
to hear it howl
for the touch of a woman.

My Muse

Kelvin is my muse–
he sends me emails
when I'm down,
about meeting a girl
with a tongue like an eel,
rugby jokes,
and getting caught up
in the most wonderful
lap dancing bar.

I send him dark poems,
and he replies
'Need a kebab?
We played five-a-side and
pestered the local virgins,
no bloody drugs,
two damn hours driving
to Chelmsford.'

I send him sad poems
he replies 'Meet me'
and then says seriously
as he sprints up the steps
'Feel my buns
I have been working out, and
I have found a man for you,
an accountant from Guyana
You could have a good time–
you need a good time.'

That's O.K. Kelvin
you show me there is
a Good Time World,
that exists
away from words,
this I need to know,
my muse.

Spanish Sun

I sit waiting in the hospital
as we all have skin cancer.
We are older now
than when we sat in Marbella.

You lot stayed at the Hilton,
I can see by the rings on your fingers
clenched like leather claws,
mottled with long fingertips.

I slept under the pine trees,
and listened to Paco's guitar.
I got sick on too much Anis
said I stayed at 'Los Pinos'.

But now we are all equal,
for thirty-five years ago
we shared in
the cruel and majestic
Spanish sun.

Vanunu

For every click of your camera
your film portrayed for us
those dials, and phials, and buttons,
that plutonium, and radium, and uranium.

What were those words?
That poem that you wrote
in haste, on your fingers,
and then rubbed off in fear.

You put your prison shoes on,
shoes going nowhere.
You looked down on them
every day for eighteen years,
your mind recoiling,
every day,
from that idea of nowhere.

For every click
they made you pay
with months of blunt silence,
they made you pay
for showing us the truth.

And yet your humanity
looked up, always,
over your bowed head,
as we look up to you,
then and now,
selfless Vanunu.

It Was All My Fault

As soon as we met,
I felt I had come home.
Safety, the thing I did not know
(I wasn't in love, but I needed you.)

Ha, the Head Boy
meets the suspended girl.
You at your cricket nets
with a red ball of twine.
(I didn't even make the softball team.)

Singing in the boys choir,
you must have been pretty,
with your downy English face.
(While I in the dusty colonial pile,
failed to hit the high C.)

Your drove our cars so well,
the orange, the silver, the brown
Lancia, the symbol of our divorce.
I told you not to buy it, the ugly brute
as the engine slid out.
(I am still on Shank's pony.)

I sat in the pub,
drinking new minted money
I said, 'Come here beside me',
patting the red banquette
in the Hen and Chickens.
(While the Cock brooded over the road.)

Now your hands are worn,
I held them, working for another woman.
I said, I would not let this happen, shame,
it will be your ruin, come sit beside me
(and drink, drink the poison away.)

Ireland

Her inky Irish curls
and large blue eyes
stilled in the air suddenly,
and she said earnestly
'I was twelve, and
there was this bomb, and
as I lay injured on the ground,
my neighbour's head,
Mr. George Travers,
rolled towards me,
and rested
near my hand.'

Voices

I hear the people in my street,
their cockney accent
jocular, proud, belonging.
I do not know them,
but know them.
They are in the tapestry of me
woven on the underside,
so you cannot see them.

Like the old women in the dark well
of an apartment building in Barcelona,
their interminable voices
striding the air like a thick funnel
biting at the windows,
the strength of their being.

This is what we miss, what is absent,
when the land grieves,
when we all know silence,
in that silence the devil sings,
the birds are stilled,
and animals lie down,
but the machines keep on,
bluntly doing for us.

I can still hear my happy banter
in the Muslim wood yard,
on nine eleven, when the devil sang,
and they glumly watched the television
above the hammers and the saws.
I did not see the screen–
I saw reflected, in their sorrowed eyes
myself abstracted
as the gay and simple past.

Camden

The man and woman are having a domestic,
a room-sized fight with animal screaming
at the full extent of their sound,
echoing through the Camden trees.

He is out and walking shirtless past the police,
saying, 'I am not having that,
the bitch tried to stab me in the arse!'
He tries to drive away, but he cannot,
it is not the sitting down–
his wheel is clamped.
'It is a crime trying to park around here,'
the neighbours mutter.

Wave

I rang my grown child's mobile
on the outer edge of the earth,
on Boxing Day.
I keened for her voice,
I feared the space of the world.

She said breathlessly,
'We are having a barbecue on the beach,
but the sky is horrible, the day is
so dark and strange.'

The young people sounded
awed and frightened,
far-off on the foreign sand.
So I was passed around,
amongst strange children,
but still a mother,
in a small telephone.

As up the welling wave reared
on a far shore,
sucking at their senses,
a sea so gloating in its massiveness
to gorge itself on
another poor mother's lovely ones.

Far Away

Your sob is taken by satellite
I hear its echo in a mean room.
I feel keenly those thousands of miles
that separate us–
remember my arms in my voice,
remember my strength.

I think of the big aeroplane
I would need to get to you
as some monster, it's belly filled
with sleeping soft bodies
grinding over immense plains,
vast mountains, great lakes of Africa,
sunrise sunset, world enormous.

How I hate you all, monstrous
lands, oceans between us, as
my spirit is propelled up to the stars
and down to you.
You must stop crying,
for I am so dreadfully impotent,
so far away.

Beloved

My beloved blood it has been too long
I see your slender neck, I need you back,
it has been too long, I feel bereft.

I know we have felt anger
constrained together
your stuff, my stuff
you have been away.

Where
water leaps in diamond fall
into black hollows
seen by tigers only.
Frond tipped trees
spread their soft leaves
under an aching sky
brilliant birds swoop
     and nothing moves below
in mountains of grey shale
where the fur-petal flower
of ancient seed
is a pin-point of pink and yellow
against the harsh stone.

Walking in the City

One summer morning,
as the sun came up over London,
I walked the deep clefts,
past the still flanks, past
the white Portland flesh.

I wondered whether I will ever be
a part of this, or feel that
this sightless giant on his side,
in the emptiness,
will suddenly wake,
and crush my puny foreign self?

Who dares walk alone
between these haunches,
of this old monster,
who is pretending to be asleep,
and not so cruel.

Oh London, on a Sunday,
stay the dreamed of town,
let me not tire of you,
do not drag me down.

Just be beautiful, quiet and white,
dormant, on this summer morn,
so grand in the warm sunlight.

The Northern Wind

Outside away from gaiety
and the sweaty throng,
I gasp at the hard cold slab of air,
as I walk the pavement long.

I know you come from some mountain lair,
so high in Scotland, blasting me from there,
so clear, so sharp, so cold,
so strong, so like a rapist's hold.

Only some balding heather breeds
on your angry brow,
no furtive chicks dare seek a brothy bow
off your craggy heap, nor do I need you now,
you breathing in my face– yes, Northern wind
freeze my breath, claw my fingers clenched below,
us Southerners do know,

Antarctica can freeze my marrow hot,
has killed your brave adventurous Scot,
and so, to my Antarctica's bleak cold face
you, the Northern wind, will bow.

A Country Childhood

Was it countryside, or some vast suburb?
Of wooden box houses,
creaking metal washing lines,
straggling rose bushes,
with the smell of cows
and sleeping horses
under a wide expanse of blue sky.

As wide and clear as loneliness.

That was countryside,
where you made the games mad,
grasping the electric fence for a dare,
running barefoot amongst the brambles,
jumping from the milk-shed roof,
for a slight taste of death.

Getting lost on your bike,
miles and miles away,
with strange men whistling
like ghosts, to frighten you,
as if on a fairground ride.

Yes, the boredom made it countryside,
everybody knew everybody else.
They were watching you, until
you managed to get away.

Yes, you got away.

The Stream

As a child, you walked me home
along miles of gravelled road,
sweet sunlit paths,
alone I trod.

I would have kissed the gravel
for a comic to buy,
reading in my tree-top lair,
and to buy a bottle of magic–
the first sip full of stars.

Instead, I heard the birds calling,
the animals knowing I was there.
Thirsty, I bent to drink from the stream,
and thought I tasted roots, stones, sharp moss,
but no, it was the silence of the simple world.

For you have been a stalwart friend
checked my excesses, taught me well,
your teachings were perfect, oh one I cannot see
always at my side, dear Poverty.

The Lamplighter

I was walking him to the station,
the last lamplighter.
He was as rigid walking
as the pole he used to carry–
so amongst the Soho revelry
he did not want to tarry.

I faltered on the cobbles
of Soho Street and thought,
'Oh God, we are all going to die.'
A young man gripped my hand
like a wick lighting me, his palm hot and high
with the strength of his youth
'Good on you, girl,' he said.
I would have followed him to the stars
and lit up the night, to be young and uncouth.

Old Stephen said, his eyes as black as soot
'It is better I walk by myself,'
and turning into a silken bat
stepped on with elbows out, and
routed the figures around him,
as they moved white, in a stupor,
like smoke around a taper.

Oh God, he is going to die
the gaslight no more is shining
this might be our last goodbye
why do I feel such a failing?

But our streetlight shadows
danced gaily along the street
like the last eerie living thing,
and in the underground we promised
that tomorrow we would bring
new words, and Death could wring
his hands, and choose another.

Night Bus

As the night bus charges
through the spattered streets
I watch the look of despair
as the e and the alcohol
leaves the youth facing me–
his face wan under rat-tails.

His dead mother comes to me,
and says, 'He is my darling boy–
touch his trembling eyelids
and sad mouth for me.'
But the bus just hurtles on
through the spattered streets.

His mother's tears cry, cry,
over the windows wet,
gutters greedy take the rush,
we are all as one
as the night bus takes her son,
me, and the rat-tails
through the spattered streets.

Kentish Town

A man meets a boy
in my street.
'Where is your brother?'
He asks the boy.
'At home inside, asleep.'
He answers.
'No he is not, I know,
he is inside, isn't he?'
'No he is not, he is asleep.'
'He might be, but I know,
he is Inside.'

The Master of Ceremonies

He had bearing, the Master of Ceremonies,
he had been on the best American cruise ships,
but now there was fear in his old man's eyes.
He said, 'I will buy food
and hurry to the mountains,
I am afraid.'

In his little New York apartment
he had looked downtown,
and then turned his back on the unfamiliar,
aghast, then turned back again,
hoping for the familiar,
his eyes retreating from the sight–
the absence of the known.

And this other old man,
gazing in shock at the dust
of his mother's house,
the emptiness filled with the cruising tread
of the Israeli tanks, turning street by street,
led by the Master of Ceremonies.

In Rwanda, this old man
sees blank terror in the you
of his family,
hacked y and o
lie on the ground,
there is only u
as cheering mobs ravage,
directed by
the Master of Ceremonies.

See in sweet Beslan
there is a new Headmaster–
he holds every attention,
and the greatest anguish known to man.
The burly fathers crouch
armed, impotent,
to be near the death of their babies,
for the black widows remember
the Master of Ceremonies.

Charnel houses, charnel houses,
and now in London Town so dear,
Death stalks Algate, King's Cross,
and rides the Number thirty
to lovely Tavistock Square.

Now sitting next to you
is a vainglorious young man.
He plots a death for two
or all, that he can hurt
for glory in his fevered brain
will be his last and terrible fine concert,
to be forever glossed in black and white.
For the Master of Ceremonies
rides within us all, and power
needs to assert, as we cower,
and forget the civil right.

Armed

He was sitting next to me on the bus
riding fast up to Camden.
'Old soldier, talk to me'.
he answered,
'I live in Tavistock Square,
and there were pieces of people
all over the road, red hands, arms,
moans of despair.'
His face was set and pale,
being English of the old school,
so passive, so cool.
I, not English born,
Said 'Give me that young murderer
here, let him be in front of me
with his bomb lust,
and I will strangle him
with my bare hands, now, on this bus.'

Relief coloured his face
and moistened his eye
I stood up and we shook hands,
we said a heartfelt goodbye,

and he took my empty place.

Struggle

I struggle, lifting my feet out of the bog
sucking at my deadened footsteps,
until I lie down in despair,
crunching my teeth in anxiety.
Connections are lost. Everything is blank.
Flicker on, flicker off.

I could always try the alcohol, the great
mad balloon, that takes me high,
winging through great gusts of cloud,
fast, faster over the sighing bay,
as I look down at myself
and say,

'I pity your struggle, oh Sober One,
and your trials never ending,
but I am damn pleased
you will earn this buck,
that I am spending.'

Lash

Fifty and not out my dear friend Chris
a day and party I cannot miss
more sunny days outside the French
we will lash the booze, and the thirst we'll quench.
In Gerry's our spirit will not be marred.
Walking the morning dew, we will be silly
and chase the pigeons
in empty Piccadilly.

Sunflower

Vincent, I read your paintings well,
I can understand your thoughts
as you paint.
But if we were at
two easels in the sunflower field,
you would paint
in the Knowledge of God,
full of the Love of Him.

Now if I painted the same scene,
I would paint mindful of
the chaos of empty creation,
the march of remorseless decay,
and the relentless formation
of the Uncaring Void.

I am but a fragment of this star,
a troubled mote between the drift.
You believe in Church and Hall,
and so with broken sunflowers
and bloody fingertips,
you will have to fall.

Regent's Park

In a crowd, when next to you,
I feel a rightness, when together.
I feel solid like an animal,
complete, not needing words.

Love does not have to cross my brow,
for a few moments together,
is enough, to feel more right–
when everything else is wrong.

It is a small picnic on the grass
set under a shaded tree,
on a hot summer Sunday
in Regent's Park.

It is the quick kisses of a child
before squirrels are chased,
and you lie there, letting the sun
take away the thought of wasps.

It is the twilight pansies, now
warm and furred like a rabbit's ear,
as strange as a Martian's face,
as dark as the coming night.

It is the flower's centre, a yellow eye
showing me, for here is truth so real,
surely we will never be,
your breath in mine, was just a dream
one moment of chance
I did but steal.

The Turning Tree

If I could get to
the Turning Tree,
I would be so slim,
and happy, and stop
drinking so much, leave him,
have my teeth fixed,
and wear smart clothes, in wool-mix.

I would not get lost, anymore, at all.
Blind now, I would see like a tiger–
hear my footfall!

Yes, I would be there,
then I could see,
at last,
the Turning Tree.

Tower Block

I looked out on London
as the sun rose,
a swollen sullen boy.

I wanted to love you,
but your horizon was
a twinkling grey scar,
full of a sleeping silent mass,
who denied the forests.

It got me to thinking–
perhaps I could leave you,
London, one day.

Whitebait

I wanted to talk to somebody
about buying
the bank down the road.

I wanted to say,
How nice it was,
to see humanity pass by,
on the sunlit street.

But I was stood up.

I bought some whitebait,
and their little fried eyes
looked at me,
and said, 'Hello,
you stupid prick.'

Cut-Out

I walked around a corner,
arm in arm with a friend,
and then suddenly I saw you
leaning on a lamppost,
lost in my street,
drunk in the rosy twilight,
a cut-out man
in a Victorian swap-book.

I am flesh and blood,
and as I saw you in that instant
I knew I was in love
with an impossibility–
it will hurt,
I will see your scissor mouth
say those scissor words,
feel my flesh sag, my blood still,
for I am real, but I will walk through,
arm in arm with a friend.

An English Field

If I die, perhaps here in London, it will be,
though born in Parnell, under a shady fern-topped tree,
where brackish mangrove water swirls,
and harsh songs come from whirling gulls,
where purple volcanoes cough up scoria,
as we glumly watch *South Pacific*
in the dark downtown Victoria.

Shall I lie there in tunnelled clay?
Will I get old and return one day?
Or will I make this London a mongrel place,
and not even dead downwards face,
to look at my far off land?
Not buried by my people's hand,
if I have a people, at all, if here I stand?

Oh, I wish I could sail high above those lonely sunlit hills,
and smell the pure earth of that strange place,
with just the trees, those insects and birds again,
and not be our base animal matter, our destructive frame.

Now to be burned and scattered
over England's frozen shore,
so then England will not be England, anymore.

St George flag

It was there in your name, Stoneman,
so Jewish to American ears–
but No, you said, it was the name
of the man who weighed the stones, collected the taxes
for the early roads in Devon.
And so you delt out things, right, careful.
You said, It is the status quo,
as I fought the stranglehold of marriage.

Once there was another couple in war-blunted Devon,
poets under creeping forest, black sulking hills,
with the stump-wart people,
who would have smelt out the Hun in her,
like sows with a tree-root.
You with your dough faces
stuck in the pinched-pie of ancient hurts,
you marry us for the glimpse of wide open sky,
but all there is, a yawning divide, a chasm–
so I wanted to punch and punch
because the English are always right,
and we are always wrong.

You asked for my hand
in front of all your pompous friends
I felt like a deer in headlights, and
they laughed when I said No, and cried,
Don't worry, Bingo
don't ask her again, she might say yes.
And they were right, and I was wrong.

And yet, and yet
I now wake in a friend's flat,
here I see a puny St. George flag
embraced with red on white
seemingly bowed in shame,
some relic of a rugby match
and think of my Great Grandfather,
with his Norfolk Volunteers,
killing, destroying, hanging
from Pretoria to Liechtenstein–
St. George tattooed on his back.
Big ants in Africa I retorted,
angry at my mothers boasting
that he would never have felt the lash.

And yet, yet again, in the morning frost,
I hear a cockney bellow down Weighhouse Street,
a medieval sound that pulls me through the centuries–
this sound like a stone hurtling through deepest space
rent from the London Wall- these things, this flag, this
   sound,
so much stronger than I–
or was I part of some strange agenda?
That diluted that strength as I lie
in a bright new day
in this country with no parliament.

To Seamus Heaney

You male poets
have taught me things,
your real love of wives,
and your enjoyment of driving
in the country.

Then, suddenly, your little god
peeps up from your words
so I can taste
with my mind's tongue
your man-brain,
and strange bristling chin.

Like Me

Like me, you found an Englishman
you thought the handsomest.
Like me, you had a daughter
who wove gold in your hair.

Like me, the man left you,
the weight of you too heavy
for his panting heart.

Like me, you explored
the black spaces your father left you,
that he should have filled with light.

I meet your daughter,
and see the shadow of you
across her brow.
But, as in my daughter
I see the love of you both
in her sturdy bones.

Poesy

If with gracious curlicues my words to lie,
and with Dryden's pall my words to brake,
to fashion's meter, rhyme and iambics high,
to purse my lips, for poesy's tight sake,
my coarse blood would still, and in poesy's grand hall,
my tiny voice might stumble,
and yet blindly silent fall.

Poetry Reading

I said to her
after his poetry reading,
'You wouldn't want to
shag him,
mindful of his poem
of making love
to a woman
long ago, as
you might turn up
in one of his poems.'

'At the very least,'
she replied,
'your fanny would!'

Chuff

I was looking after a cat
in a flat in the Charing Cross Road,
when a young man was
beaten to death outside.
His blood ebbed away
as the sirens wailed.

In the morning
the street cleaning vehicle
coughed along
in the silent street–
it was like it had never happened.

Except for his family who wailed
somewhere, not here,
the air heavy with the absence
of their grief,
as the busy sightless machine
proclaimed chuff, chuff, chuff,
in the quiet morning air.

Love at First Sight

Love is the softening of the marrow
of your old and bitter bones,
and the waiting of the tiger,
panting, watchful,
amongst the river stones.

So too the widow spider, in her furry dell,
awaiting the spangled butterfly,
whose beating wings will spell
the destruction of her careful web,
spun softly from her lonesome thigh.

Feel the waiting of the baby twin
as the storm clouds roll darkly in,
abandoned on the bleak hillside,
by her who never will abide.
She the only mother that she knows,
so hurt do hide, and eyes now close.

Change and damnation she did bring,
accident, collision, so go lick
the wounded heart,
and savour the awakened thought–
that this fearsome love
did make you so sad, and oh so sick.

This hurt that you yourself did make
in others, they felt this way.
So be as strong as the ploughman's brake
and save yourself, for love and care
shall come, on a more auspicious,
clear, and sensible day.

Kentish Town Tree

Often I watched the doves in your soft foliage,
and the squirrels flying on your branches,
like clutching grey gloves.
You seemed so aloof to the high houses,
we hemmed you in with our straight city shadows,
but in you, the memory of farmland held,
and gently the Fleet ran past, down
to the Thames, little river,
now sightless, guttered into a sewer.

I see men swinging on your massive frame,
and soon machines are screaming at your bulk.
The saws bite and the shredding machine
makes you palatable for small gardens.
The ugly pale lilandii, squat fat, foreign,
will grow even taller, untamed,
free from under your native shadow,
the natural order is now gone–
the air is where you were, and the birds that knew
your safe spaces so well,
keep away, they keep away.

I feel a great sense of wrongness.
We can't go on like this, making space,
making space for us, the swarming city.
You must have been two hundred years old,
and in the way of us, now chopped up,
just fit for garden mould.

Ant Heads

I went past the pub in the bus,
it was revving up for the hill-too fast,
I saw the black ant-heads of men,
no chance of defining you
against the golden bar light,
behind the driving rain.

I am sorry about the cancer,
but if I stop and get off,
I will unravel the years,
and I would walk in
like a drowned monkey,
and have to pretend
to be just passing,
if you were not there.

To a Child of Suicide

Selfish is not a word
that lives in the mind of suicide,

except perhaps
as a soft scoop of pack ice,
that drifts from Antarctica–
ice-cream of nothingness,
but still, complete, unseen,
above acres of blue, then
dark murky green–

then blackness, total blackness–
but – here are creatures
unnamed, warm, floating in the spew
from inner earth, the violent cauldron,

and far above; the pulsating star,
years away, heavy with time,

but like us, a mote, a fleck
of ash, God brushes
from his serge lap,
as he smokes
his fat cigar.

Hazlitt's Hotel

Snug in the four-poster, we talked to nearly dawn,
then black Dog fell asleep.
His snoring was so loud that
Hazlitt's ghost came out of the wall,
wearing a neat green jacket, looking prim,
and rather disdainful.

I felt offended and said to him,
'Well anyway I have read,
that your landlady here
pushed a dead tenant under the bed,
to let the room again!'
He ignored me and just asked
'Why is he called Black Dog,
when he is white'?

'Because he used to own one', I replied.
He looked annoyed, and suddenly disappeared.
Black Dog woke up, and I said laughing,
'Your snoring would awaken the dead–
it couldn't be louder,
and now I have met my favourite writer!'

Lilies

A sunny Sunday afternoon, in Kentish Town,
with the peals of St Michael's gone.
On the pavement a man lies stabbed–
are there lilies on his chest?
No, it is white gauze,
and he is on a stretcher–
butterflies of white on his naked chest.
The plastic mask falls from his face
as he lies there.

A shape turns above him
and says to me
'My life has been full and grand,
my family good and strong, tell them'.
'I don't know who he is', I murmur.
The old Irish lady at my shoulder says,
bowing to the man,
'I do-not that I drink in pubs, mind.'
then added–'What a terrible thing
to happen on a Sunday!'

And so lilies not dandelions came to Kentish Town,
as six black horses led the black carriage down.

Torture

The small brown man stopped me
with the lightest touch,
and asked where
the Medical Centre
for Torture Victims was.
I pointed to the proper doorway,
but he ran away into the betting shop,
and hid from me,
behind the baying betting throng.

Yellow and Orange

I was sick again, so mother said put on
your sick pyjamas,
from your grandmother.
So I lay in the lemon orchard with
the lemons above me, vomit yellow,
held in their space, so smooth, so cool.
Not I in the yellow pyjamas,
woolsick, prickly sick,
curled up in sickly heat.

The boys in Vietnam
saw orange trees with their orange eyes–
collateral damage in a sick war,
and the dominoes did not fall.
They were spots in our eyes
and the yellow men won,
even as we turned their trees,
their women, their children, orange.

So now men must hate the colour orange,
as they are sick in their orange pyjamas,
as I hate the colour yellow,
as we are sick, sick, sick.

Lansdowne Club

So restful, opulent, so confident,
so English, those cornices, and fireplaces,
the very fire confident.
I feel more at home than he does, though, the member,
his Irish scrapes the varnish off the table
But now I see it suddenly, this place is built
on the backs of slaves.

Published

The book grew inside me, now I felt lovelorn
I had let it be doctored, and then slowly born.

There it lies so quiet, just a sleeping head
in swaddling clothes, with closed eye–
as I wait in dread
for its first mewling cry.

Dulled, and with a postnatal sigh,
I go out, and gamely buy
a lamp of sparkle lustre, a crown,
droplets of red crystal jewellery,
to stop me coming down.

I take it on a crazy dance
of drinking, but keep it safe,
it is a symbol, a silent carapace.

Watching the night cab's meter
homeward, I keep it close,
a present for a new author,
my bare room to juxtapose.

But still dank-damned in Dogwood
I see the lamp now resembles
globules of dried blood,
instead of glamour, fine theatre,
and my very own selfhood.

Kentish Town Night

The trees spit above the cats,
under the cars, over the stones,
and baby sleeps on his white pillow,
embroidered 'Gary'
as black cabs purr, throwing out
crystals of yellow light.

Curved Edwardian lampposts
gracefully lean to the past.
Foxes, eyes pricked bright
careless, unheeded foxes
rip black plastic bags
and the white skin
of a burst chicken.

Brakes

He rang up breathless
as his brakes had failed
on twelve miles of hairpin bends-
then he drove into a wall to stop.
He said, 'Come and live with me.'

Would the blind fish
in the stargazey pie, grin,
to see us lie under an American moon?
Would the Devil spin
at glaciers melting so soon?
Would he be startled, agape,
to see us return, to our family shape?

For now our stargazey dreams
-forever stuck by the tail-
echo with soul, in a vast golden hall,
as the lights flicker off, in the storms that rail,
full of angry sleet and salt,
across lovely Mousehole.

El Puerto de Santa Maria

I thought I would shut the metal grill again,
and we would walk down Calle Cielo again,
with the bells pealing, and you always saying,
'Mind the cars, Ally', as we stepped and stopped
at quiet bars, to the smell of the sea.

I said, 'Don't you die on me now.'
Then, pleased, you stood up and slammed coins on the bar
and cried 'Dos cerveza!' with a wide grin.

Pain disappeared for a moment and Spanish time stood still,
and in the bay the little ferry tooted for passengers
as your boat came sailing in.

Opening

On the coffee packet was the word familial
I tried to open the foil
from the side, a beak, a spout,
but it opened –unfamiliar–
in the middle, a coffee-mouth opened.

Ha, the sublime difference of thinking
said, 'Here, smell Paris again.'

Pegs on the line.

That line next door,
a tattered monument to domesticity.
Once you must have pegged up clothes, absent minded.
Absent you are, and those bodies, now absent,
those baby clothes–
and the pegs grip at nothing in the wind
in a row, like little people, but
all hands are down,
delivered
to the wind.

Night Troubled

I quietly tramp the streets of North London,
the Angel, the Cross, the Town
curving away from me, the windows
black, the people silent, curled in their beds,
their eyelashes fluttering with dreams
as I step, step on these cobbles, worrying.

As the miles pass, the answer comes to me
I am selling land away from my blood forever–
but surely it is life itself that is the precious gift?

Dawn comes as the warm birds stir high in the plane trees
and I know that London is a grey crust of stone,
above a meadow, on a blue planet, and
we are but soft insects in its shell
hurtling around, and around, and around.

Girl

You are a bit dependant,
and try and get into my bed,
under the covers,
and you are fussy about what you eat–
you love packet ham that smells of preservative,
and stare at my boyfriends,
as if to say, 'Go on, show us, that you are a jerk.'

But you are pretty, and quiet,
and after twelve years together, we know
each other's faults–
and that, I guess, is all
a friend should be
as we lie here,
my pussycat and me.

Christopher

We talked of balustrades, of spindles
flat roofs and cladding.
Of hanging joists,
basements, and pipes,
and wet rot, and lagging.

But when I saw you naked,
Christopher, not telling tales,
himself
was in the details.

Street Tree

I am leaving my home forever–
in the corner of my eye, through the window,
the street tree waves a frantic warning.

'What are you saying tree?'
You seem so natural, free
–not snapped, not broken by casual violence.
But then you are rooted in this street,
I have seen you grow from a sapling.

But perhaps your seed shall hide itself
in the chassis of the car beneath you,
to be stolen, and sold in parts, in Nigeria.
So you will grow again, on some dusty track.

Then somehow your seed will fly back, like me
to grow into another London tree, like you,
and when I pass beneath
you will whisper to me
of *Africa!*